# RIVER TIME

Piscataqua Press
Portsmouth, New Hampshire

# RIVER TIME

WRITING FROM THE SNAKE RIVER
HELLS CANYON
2023 FISHTRAP OUTPOST

ARROWLEAF BALSAMROOT
Balsamorhiza sagittata

## RIVER TIME
## IS DEDICATED TO
## JANIE TIPPETT

Janie Tippett belongs to this canyon and its river, this lifting place; it calls to her like love. We dedicate *River Time* to Janie. She chose to celebrate her 90th birthday here with all of us. Her party went long into the night with singing and stories and Kelsey Juve's chocolate stout cake. Janie was the first awake and up in the mornings, a de facto teacher and guide all day, and not the first to head to her tent at night. She and her stories are full of joy, wisdom, and humor. It is an honor to be in her presence. May this book of ours remind us that what truly matters is, as Janie says, "I'm in the moment." *Mary Anker*

Janie Tippett made me laugh every day and made me cry once. Her writing was always fresh and wise and unexpected (like Janie herself) and one day a particular observation in a piece she was sharing reached me so deeply that I felt tears spring to my eyes. Wow, I wish that I had her powers. Or her energy. Or her boyfriends! Janie knows how to live. This world would be a better place if everyone followed her lead. Janie, please make a podcast called *Janie Knows How to Live*. And thank you for all the smarts and joy and love you shared with us. *Beth Piatote*

# INTRODUCTION

Sometimes we find ourselves somewhere and assume it's part of our planning. Then at a widening moment, a leaning simultaneously inward and outward, a dawning. Like rafts approaching rapids. Secure in our strategy until the swoop. Hells Canyon. The Snake River. Fishtrap Outpost. Winding Waters River Expeditions. Turning points.

The writing within *River Time* is a result of opening ourselves to an opportunity that encourages, allows, maybe even demands that we dig in and let go. The canyon is mind-blowing. Vast and full of faces. River, sky, flora, fauna, symbiotic and gorgeous. Humans. Unnecessary.

But humans we are, hanging out with the river, swimming upstream then muscling into the eddy, letting it carry us back to camp. Scaling heights while stopping to look, identify, taste. Writing around a table by the river's edge. Falling asleep on warm rocks.

Beth Piatote's first assignment asked us to introduce ourselves to the land with wonder, care, and connection. "Every living thing in the canyon, in our world, is our relative." Her prompts led us deep into the canyon and its history. She taught us words in the Nez Perce language. Here is an example of the spelling and morphology of the Nez Perce word for friends, lawtiwa: law = fish, and tiwa = mate, lawtiwama = friends.

Janet Hohmann turned us into keen and curious naturalists. She walked humbly with us. It felt as though she was giving us a tour of her house. Her encyclopedic knowledge was always presented with, "I think it could be this, but I may be wrong." She was never wrong. She taught us the language of trees, flowers, weeds and their history and purpose.

How lucky we were to have these river guides, led by Robin Pace, who let the river thrill us. Guides sense the moods of the river. They taught us to pay attention and read the water and its surroundings. Swoop, tongue, seam, eddy... became our vocabulary. They nourished us and our spirits. These five young adults turned us into family. All eighteen of us wrote for this anthology. That's a statement.

Awakening to river time became the philosophical underpinning of a trip turned pilgrimage. A circle of lawtiwama who wrote and read and listened, who knew finally that what they found was the plan.

Mary Anker, Editor

# FROM OUR TEACHERS AND GUIDES

## Beth Piatote

First of all, I wish to express my deep gratitude to the amazing group of writers—not only the participants but also the guides—who contributed such grace, beauty, and energy to the trip. It was an honor to spend that week on the river with you, to learn from you, and to laugh, row, and pee in the river with you. Special thanks to the wonderful guides for keeping us alive on the river and indulgently fed and sheltered on shore. Much gratitude to Mary Anker for editing this sweet volume. So much love to everyone! As the writing instructor for Outpost on the Snake River, my aspirations were twofold: to provide some structure that would invite the flow of writing, and to not get in the way of the river. To not mess with river time. To let the river bring the words.

## Janet Hohmann

My goals as naturalist on this trip were to: 1) integrate my experience and knowledge with Beth's "lesson plan", and 2) add to everyone's enjoyment of and writing about the river. Hells Canyon has cast its spell on me, and I would venture to guess that it has done the same for you. I'd like to think that I assisted in that spellcasting. And I must thank each and every one of you for welcoming me into your group and enhancing my river time.

## Robin Pace

Below are my "goals" for our trip together, and every trip. Thanks for riding with me!!

River trips are more than whitewater, lounging in the river, really good food, and starry nights. Every trip is a story we are lucky enough to write together, and hopefully vulnerable enough to remain present for the reading. Story moves through all of us, bubbles to the surface, bounces off and into each of our lives and one another. I believe in story and the way it weaves us all together into place. The way it reminds us we were not the first to walk among these canyon walls, just like the river running through it was not the first water to kiss its rocks, because first there was salt–an ocean of it. A little salt: makes every Dutch oven cake taste a little sweeter, helps keep the body hydrated, drips from a brow, seeps from a tear duct, stains cloth and earth alike. Salt and story remind us we are part of this earth, and therefore part of each other. Every river trip is its own, the trick is to listen to it, let it be, and move with it; just like dancing a boat downriver.

# CHOCOLATE STOUT CAKE
## Made by Kelsey Juve for Janie Tippett's 90th Birthday Party

Editor's note: It had been a rainy day. The tarp was up. The night was pitch-dark. We could taste and smell the cake, but not see it. These circumstances added to its delectability and to the celebratory atmosphere. We decided to include this recipe in our chapbook so that we can bring that time back whenever we want. Thank you, Kelsey, for this recipe and for your diligence, positive outlook, presence, and talent.

This recipe originates from King Arthur Baking Company

## Ingredients:

- 2 cups (454g) stout or dark beer, such as Guinness
- 32 tablespoons (454g or 1 pound) unsalted butter, cold
- 1 1/2 cups (128g) Dutch-Process Cocoa
- 4 cups (480g) King Arthur Unbleached All-Purpose Flour
- 4 cups (794g) granulated sugar
- 1 tablespoon baking powder
- 1 1/2 teaspoons table salt
- 4 large eggs, at room temperature
- 3/4 cup (170g) sour cream, at room temperature

## Directions:

1. Preheat the oven to 350°F. Grease and flour three 8" or two 9" cake pans, and line them with parchment paper circles or reusable pan liners. Be sure your 9" pans are at least 2" deep.

2. **To make the chocolate stout cake:** Place the stout and butter in a large, heavy saucepan, and heat until the butter melts. Remove the pan from the heat and add the cocoa powder.

3. Whisk until the mixture is smooth. Set aside to cool to room temperature.

4. Whisk together the flour, sugar, baking powder, and salt in a large bowl; set aside.

5. In a large mixing bowl, beat together the eggs and sour cream.

6. Add the stout-cocoa mixture, mixing to combine.

7. Add the flour mixture and mix together at slow speed. Scrape the sides and bottom of the bowl, and mix again for 1 minute.

8. Divide the batter equally among the prepared pans. (The recipe yields about 10 cups or 2625g of batter. If you're making a double-layer cake, each pan should have about 5 cups or roughly 1312g. If you're making a triple-layer cake, each pan should have about 3 1/3 cups of batter or 875g).

9. Bake the layers for 40 to 45 minutes for 8" pans, or 55 to 60 minutes for 9" pans, until a cake tester inserted into the center comes out clean. Remove the cakes from the oven and cool on a rack for 10 minutes before turning the cakes out of their pans and returning to the rack to finish cooling completely before frosting.  According to Kelsey, frosting not really needed and wasn't used for Janie's cake.

# CONTENTS

**MARY ANKER**

**prompt:  this is the time of life when...**

a friend hands us a stone
and a husband says go
let the river be heard

rusted rake and bed springs
rising moon
close relatives

especially that stone
green-brown with old lichen-orange flecks

like the nutrient bubbles
floating alongside
our raft

# Prompt: Prose Poem about a Small Being

When I see half-moon and her million attending stars brilliant above, I long to sleep outside. I obsess. I know others are out there. Night after night. Undaunted.

In limbo, I sit half-in/half-out of my tent. Darkness comes gently in this valley of depth. At first, the gorge fades pink as only its crests loom backlit, jagged, and eerie. Wild sage strong as the heat cools. The chill alive. The Snake echoes below our river bench. The last of everyone settles in. I'm alone among the tents. Hells Canyon. Geology. On my mind. And fear.

Here the lightest of small beings startle me. Scare me at first if I admit it. A white swarm in the strobe of my headlamp. I calm myself. Switch off the lamp. Quivering before take-off, they tell me what I already know: fear is a sorry thing. My lack of courage berates me. Weary from my internal debate, I move inside. Zip only the outside flaps to let in the wind.

I'm up and out at first light. My fear, a tiny being this morning. I see Sarah's mother asleep surrounded only by bunch grass and chokeberries. Wonder at her.

Back in New Hampshire, I look at a picture of Beth alone with the river beyond her. This image brings back those mornings and nights. From here and now, I wonder at my quivering then. Wonder how my once fearless self now shrinks from harmless beings, from a quiet dark, from a world no crazier than it has ever been.

**prompts: a list poem, a praise poem, a plant poem**

**praise the Western Sunflower**
   *for Janet Hohmann*

you hold your own among
eastern florist exotics
your deep golden-rayed flowers
and miracle seeds
survive and defy history's erasure

canyon, river, sky
moon and sun
your exotic terrain
you stand tall
and bright within the granite and grasses

you reside inside your daisy family

Goatsbeard     Yarrow     Hoary Balsamroot
Arrowleaf Balsamroot     Diffuse Knapweed     False Yarrow
Bull Thistle     Scotch Thistle     Gray Rabbitbrush
Gumweed     Golden Weed     Gaillardia
Fleabane Daisy     Oregon Sunshine     Little Sunflower
Dog Fennel     Groundsel     False Dandelion
Blazing Star

praise the humble Western Sunflower
longtime friend to Nez Perce
you teach us by example
*"Your flower heads face the sun throughout the day."*

**RICK BOMBACI**

## Where In Your Body Do You Carry Water?

Well, gosh, I think I must carry water in places close to where it comes out, maybe sloshing around behind my eyeballs, where it comes out at my mother's funeral or when I watch a movie about some time, some place, some person, some story that pierces me and pulls some memory, some longing to the surface.

Or maybe dripping from the end of my nose, or even gathering and drooling out of one corner of my slack mouth when relaxed but intent on some task, which a former lover used to do when playing the violin, her eyes staring off into space.

Or maybe when

## Five Questions

One. In my dreams, she is looking up at me from under the water, or I am looking at her from under the water, or we are floating or swimming next to one another and her blonde hair is slicked against her skull and her ice blue eyes slip behind mine on a causeway of love and acceptance remarkable and relieving after all these years, after I walked away from her, the love of my life.

Two. I went to the river and I asked the water where it had come from, what seep on a hillside surrounded by cheatgrass and cowshit, what trickling spring amidst meadowrue with dangling organs so small, what snags blackened in the latest burn, what snowmelt patch with glacier lilies and wild onions sprouting in the dark and moist glistening soil.

Three. I will tell the children, "This is what I learned from the river. Someday I will be gone and the river will still be here. Gravity wins in the end, pulling me toward, down to some sea I know not what but maybe a long way and maybe just around the next riffling bend."

Four. Today, this is what I say to the river, and in saying this I also say to myself: Quiet down!

Five. In the future, I will tell the river, We had some good times, you and I. Remember that July afternoon when Emily and I stood in you, up to our necks, to escape heat stroke? Remember when I sat by you for an entire afternoon in the shade of one ponderosa on a bleached and shimmering rocky plain, Eureka Bar, one hundred degrees? Well, maybe they weren't such good times, but I still like you.

Four. Today I say to the river, and in saying, also say to myself, "Buddy, you sure are going downhill!"

Three. I will tell the children, "This is what I learned from the river. The current is faster in the middle than by the shore. Jump in with both feet, but be ready."

Two. I went to the river and I asked the water to hold me up, running like a child on a mattress where dreams lay layered and deep, squeezing up between my toes, to ride the backs of sturgeon like dragons in myth time before all the engines.

One. In my dream, I am always moving always underwater no-end-in-sight no-end-in-time, rock slime against my belly, the other fish turn away or into me eye-to-eye, our mouths agape, sweet liquid pours through me, the river outside and inside me, the green light the constant hush of underwater wind, the ebb and flow of the rocks rushing by, into the past, I am still, it is still, the water we are still and the rocks fly by like butterflies on a summer breeze.

## Be Safe!

Remember walking with Jay in spring, the yellow balsamroot and gray rain clouds over Somers, finding a spot behind the ranch house at Tryon to pitch a tent and it was cold that night. A year or two later with Gee and Kay and a tin full of marijuana and mushrooms, the green of spring, and wondering where is the water going to be? Then too much water at Deep Creek which earned its name all mud brown roaring flood and no one wanted to try and fell a tree over the creek thigh high in raging current, or another time Joe that fool, again at Deep Creek going to cross in flip-flops like the young man climbing the Matterhorn in flip-flops because who knows how these people think, and Joe just thinking he's going to cross Deep Creek with a string pulling his terrified dog across the thigh high thigh high current pulling at your center of gravity, your feet wedged between the rounded greasy rocks and the awkward twisting of pained joints and all the memories of warnings Be Safe! warnings of accidents that wait for us at every turn or incidents that never happen in real real life except when they do, like that pile of rags that self-immolated and took down that five-thousand-square-foot US Forest Service visitor center one Sunday summer morning, the flames two hundred feet high.

**What Is the River Saying to You?**

Well the river, you know, is a chatterbox and won't let me get a word in edgewise, longwise, nowise. The river, she's saying, "Ha! Look at me spin! Watch me twirl! See my lacy curves of seafoam green! Am I not lovely?"

But I see, beneath the smile, a sparkling gleam of pointed tooth. "Oh, river," I say, "You are indeed lovely, and sometimes I think I love you, and always I love the sound of your voice. But you are a siren, and I will still wear my life jacket."

## MIKE COOPER

### Prompt: Find the Traces of the Ocean Around You

I always thought I'd sink the body in the Mariana Trench—wrapped tightly with stout chain, padlocks, and cinderblock. Let the pale white fish of the black abyss pick at the flesh as they do with the bodies of whales and giant squid—nothing left but baleen, bones, and beaks to be chewed between the teeth of tectonic plates.

I am at the bottom of the trench—too tall to see—carved by the water of ancient oceans, propelled by magma, deep in the hole, dark between canyon walls with nothing but a plastic paddle to keep the walls apart. My flesh belongs to the river, my bones to the gravel bars, my spirit moves downstream.

**Prompt: River Term**

## Pillow

I am three hypoallergenic pillows propped up so you can breathe
I am an inflatable Smiley Face pillow from when Smiley Faces were
cool the first time
I am the sleeve of a mink coat on a wooden church bench
I am three more pillows at the end of a sagging couch
I am a plastic suction cup pillow in the bathtub
I am the most necessary of the unnecessary
pieces of camping equipment
I am a folded towel, a stuff sack
I am the cushion of water to protect from the rock
in the middle of the river
I am synthetic, down, made of air and bubbles
I have been lain upon by puppies, kittens, children, lovers
I am sweat-stained, blood-stained, drenched in tears

**Prompt: Praise Poem for Small Being**

I give thanks to the small black flies that annoy Rick's legs
That tickle my arms and neck and the backs of my calves
Where it is not easy to reach
They know this
They have always known it

I give thanks to the parents of the small black flies
Who have so painstakingly taught their children
Through example or through epigenetics
The places to land:
At the back of the arms and legs and ears
The top of the head
Near the eyes of horse cow deer
Under the table
On the ceiling
And in the deepest woods on the hottest day
To land and bite sharply—like a hot tack
In the very middle of the backs of two shirtless boys wielding
chainsaws

I give thanks to the small black flies who have been my mother and
father
And all my children

**Sextet of Limericks for the Guides:**

There once was a talented baker
To the East Coast they said they would take her
But in the West Kelsey fit
And there were books to be writ
And pastries in need of a maker

There once was a guide name of Anders
Who goes where the river meanders
He sets up the hive
Then the duckies arrive
Like tired little gooses and ganders

There once was a woman of water
Turned out be Beth Ann's daughter
Sarah cried, "Paddles ready!"
She held the boat steady
And turned out she could swim like an otter

There once was a pirate named Clark
Who leapt rafts like a walk in the park
He boarded our boat
Took our guide for a float
As we sailed along in our ark

There once was a woman of mystery
Who shared with us all kinds of history
Robin filled us with tales
Of magma and whales
And let us re-vision the vista-ry

Each evening a tasty hors d'oeuvre
The river our guides did maneuver
They each took the reins
But one question remains:
Why is that thing called a groover?

# JACKLEEN de LA HARPE

**Prompt: Natural phenomena—weather, flora, fauna.**

## The Point of a Star

In my first memory of stars, I was hot with fever, my teeth chattering with chills and fear. *This is an emergency*, my mother said. She swaddled me tight in a pink blanket and carried me, a five-year-old chrysalis of a girl, outside into the night to our old Chevy. I knew I was in danger. I was the emergency.

The pain in my side was so intense, I could only whisper, silent tears running down my cheeks. In the darkness, everything familiar had been erased. Our house, at the end of a rutted dirt road, was surrounded by matted grass, dark woods. There were no neighbors or lights in any direction. *Look at that*, my mother whispered to me. *Look at the stars, look how beautiful.*

For a few seconds, everything froze. I saw a carpet of stars, a swath of stars, a velvety night sea of stars. It was the only thing that mattered. For that moment, I knew precisely where I was in the world, held tight and close, my fear postponed. I don't recall another thing about that night and might not have remembered it at all, had it not been for the stars.

More than six decades later, when I look at the night sky, I feel compelled to point out the constellations we all know: The Big Dipper. The Little Dipper. But my certainty starts to waver when I look for the North Star, a navigational beacon that feels, to me, unmoored and stranded. That's when I begin to drift. I might see a meteor slide across the sky. Or a satellite trudge overhead in an endless, silent orbit. But those are distractions.

I don't want the facts of stars: their names, the distance they are from Earth, why the dusty path of the Milky Way matters. I don't want mathematical equations or chemistry to dull their radiance. I don't want to put beauty in its place.

What I want is that first kiss moment when I look up to see darkness punctuated by glittering light. It's only a moment, but it's the moment that matters. *Look at that. Look how beautiful,* I'm compelled to say. Even then, I persist, keeping watch in the darkness, as if there were something, something else, to help me navigate.

I regret abandoning the stars when I close my eyes to sleep, knowing I'll forget the delicate winking of the night sky by morning. But if I forget, it will mean that I'll be taken by surprise on all the clear nights left in my life, those breathtaking few seconds when I'm rooted in place, no different than a tree or stone. Each time for a brief moment, I'll know the point of a star.

**Prompt: What does the river say to you?**

**The River Never Stops**

By morning, we crouch on the cold silt, stalling, examining the granite rocks that shift underfoot, listless, confused, my three sisters and I, our mother breaking camp, the ruined tent behind us, morning flattened by sullen light, bone-chilling mist, reluctant to roll up our sleeping bags, pack the kerosene stove, go home—the tent wall a gaping hole, we had to leave—abandon our pretend camp life for the familiar one: a house with barely enough heat, little safety, like the night before while we slept, the drunk men camping nearby, carefully unzipping the tent to look for her, our wild mother who had to protect us but couldn't protect herself, she shouting 'get out, get out', my sisters and I lying there mute, rabbits still as stone, night one form of safety and another form of danger, men climbing over us in drunken confusion to escape, darkness electric with violence, a sharp blade ripping through the canvas, icy water rushing past, the tent wall an illusion, so frail it could be slit right open like a knife tip drawn down the belly of a fish, cold useless guts tossed into a river that never stops.

**Prompt:  Write a limerick.  Wrote a haiku.**

**The course of water**

The rushing river
Finds its way to the right place
Without direction.

# BETH ANN ESTOCK

## Initiation

Slight breeze enlivens lungs.
Sun hidden, gently warms skin.
Water rolls over rocks
reverberating off canyon walls.

As if Canyon knows what I long for,
It tunes me like a singing bowl.
Body opening to its resonance.
Thoughts come
like sounds wafting through space.
Ripples in the water,
they flow downriver.

Closing eyes, the canyon rocks me tenderly.
She says, "Welcome little one, receive my medicine.
Listen. Breath. Attend.
For this is Holy Ground."

… Sky above, canyon below, water flows …
                    Embracing

I ask River to carry me
to the depths of
my pain…
          my healing…
                    my wisdom…

She says, "You need only be.
Nothing more.
Fall gently into my arms
as I sing my ancient lullaby to you."

## Batholith

Batholith, I see you.
Sun-tanned and brawny
Big-chested fortress
Standing solid through catastrophic flood
and the flow of unending time.

But in morning light you reveal
Karmas of lives past…
Stories of resilience…

Shards of angled rock
form fractals of faces.
Cacophony of expressions -
pondering, painfilled,
contorted, stretched, compacted,
inquisitive, serious, ecstatic.

You are high priestess and medicine man.
Warrior and lover,
Lion, monkey, bear.
Profiles in courage turned upward, inward, and sideways,
expanding outward beyond recognition.

Hall of Mirrors,
You are our ancestors.
You hold our secrets.
You offer wisdom.

Your primordial hum sings deep within – soul to soul.
Helping us to remember that we are
a cosmic body of divinity on this holy ground of life.
In you, we find our face.
And know we are home.

## Hackberry

I am Hackberry.
Insignificant from a distance,
I sit, crusted-green,
just beyond the shoreline of obsolescence.

But I am really a ballerina
dancing to the symphony of wind and light.
With taut, sinewy muscles
I am resilient to my core.

Pliable, I am a synthesis of both/and.
Growing upwards toward light
and then swooping down to earth.
Branches flowing in all directions.

For those who aren't easily offended
by my exotic dance moves,
You will discover my true artistry
as I reveal my corset of shade.

You're welcome.

# AMELIA DIAZ ETTINGER

## The first time I Saw the River

was the day my father showed
his seldom-seen gap-tooth smile
as he precisely parked the car

on an improbable wooden raft,
la balsa, a man with a bamboo
oar took us across the massive

waters—el Río Grande de Loiza
he told me this river held secrets of freedom,
the escape from slavery and servitude

when the Yoruba crossed its dark waters
to the thickets of mangroves that served
as curtains to the essence of Elleguá and plena dance

standing on that boat, Papi held tightly
to the door of his car, his gaze on me changed
as he spoke, his cheeks aged, they sagged

and sadness floated into his eyes,
a certainty I could not understand then,
but have been obliged to navigate

—the look that parents earn when they see
that a daughter comes of age,
and the ripples of love turn to eddies

of fear as they might seek
another passage
another wave

**Oh, it's you, Thanatos**

finally
—not that i wanted to meet you
but i always knew, of course, that you'd come
here, sit by me and tell me what it would be like,
but don't use those tiresome prosaisms
don't bore me with the light, or tunnels,

though it would be nice to see a long
receiving line of relatives—
both sides
this time, to even out
the unevenness of this life

i know you know
so set the score straight
let me visit with those that were denied
to me—go all the way
to the beginning
and start with my mother

## Kingfisher, Still Life Mount

he posed me on a tree
I don't recognize

I stand, wings splayed open
looking at my reflection

a perpetual narcissus,
on the verge of the plunge

oh, how I long for a true dive
into those northern waters

that held the anadromous
fish of the entire world,

even after the waters warmed
and the fish went stale

here in this stasis,
why did they call me King?

perhaps it was my ragged crown,
though I never had a kingdom of my own

I shared my river,
our river,

with ospreys, egrets, and rock,
now my syndactyl feet will never reach

another Panamá, another —
in this new version of me, like my eyes
water is made of glass

**in this time**

i can see the results of past thoughtlessness
and the brilliance of rewards, all learned
from a seven-year-old that opens
the world again to possibilities

like finding a bug and naming it *Lucy*
a simple orb weaver inside a Douglas fir
what a liberation from acceptance and neglect
*Lucy weaves like you knit, Nana, in perfect circles*

this child allows the erasure of narcissism
*let's build a mud cake,* his recipe
is full acceptance and joy, mud seeping
languidly between small and wrinkled fingers

this is the time when most of my life
has been lived, and his just starts
and i feel the bounty of his future,
and, incongruently, also of my past

this is the time in life when
an orb weaver can change the shell
into an ameliorated breath
*I have only two legs, Lucy has eight*

an observation that leads to riches,
exactly, exactly what we need
in this time

**KELLY FINE**

## A Pool of Deeper Sky

That shape before me—
by day I called it a towering cliff. Canyon wrens laughed
its massive face, loved every spider-roof, beaked
every crack of its rock.

Night, you hollow
the bluff, the solid

stone. A swimmer could enter
that body of dark.

No, I'm not done with the warm and wriggly dog
of Day. Cockleburs wait, and faces swollen by tears.

But years of crouching,
of cringing, have hunched me.
I want to grow brave. I am nearly old.

Night, these arms—they ache, they long,
they stretch. To slide your water, to dive.

To reach the stars that salt
your sky. Let me gather their glitter
and scrub my skin. Let me scour my skull.
Then when I gleam, let these fingertips slip
with a shimmer

to dark. As I swim
shear me clean

to the bones of this soul.
In your deep let me dream

the body to flesh them,
fresh legs to dry off, to stride me
through sun.

## Our Sap Flowing Clear

No, you said. Only simpletons could be moved by that sentimental pop. Only stunted souls, you said. But today is the sharpest autumn blue, my last morning deep in the canyon with friends. Enormous above our raft and our bodies, the shattered face of a rock wall shines. Paddles on laps, we glide the glass river. I am trying to learn a sound by heart, the cascade when our guide lifts her oars from the river, when her water returns, when it pours away. The morning still cool—and now we are singing. A startle at first, the sweet of our sound, how every voice strips the husk from another. Eight of us sing in one clear voice, eight women bright as a gleam on the river. I know the song from decades ago, when I was small and my mother was strong. My mother, age thirty, the car window open. I just want to see her. How the song moved her. If she nodded her head left and right. If she pounded the wheel with the heel of her hand. All I want is to see. Age fifty. Age sixty. Love bright as a song tears a muscle in my chest. Still we are singing our song of longing, our song for water that cannot stay. Ripples wrinkle the river that bears us. Our sorrow streams in the voice of a girl. Go ahead, call our song simple and sappy. Say I deserve less than the gush of her love. If you could hear with the ears of a daughter. If my mother could hear us deep in the canyon. Hear our song want, hear our song lift. We lift a small girl high into sunlight. Every color shimmers in her tumbling curls.

# JANET HOHMANN

## *Snake River Haiku*

Sand shakes soft from shoes;
river memories sift down.
Let us keep them close.

## There Was a Great Flood

There was a great flood of words
pouring forth from multiple sources.
Sometimes the sources originated from
a common theme, but the resulting
outpourings were dissimilar.  At other
times, the sources popped up independently,
but ended up at similar conclusions.
Regardless, the great flood was not a
thing of destruction, but rather it
was an act of creation.

**KELSEY JUVE**

**Journal Entries from the Snake River**

September 5:

In my dreams I went to the river and asked; how is your might so strong? How instead of being worn down by time you have built strength? Built enough strength to wear down stone. A constant steady flow to have made space for your vastness. To declare, I am here and here I shall remain. Oh river how are you so wise? To know so inherently the depth that you seek, the width you claim, the rate you wish to flow. I sit along your shore humbled. Of your grace, your peace. Might I find your characteristics in my lifetime? For as I sit along your shore, I sing to your attributes and sign for myself. For through my lifetime I have learned to hold space as you hold space. I will tell my children to sit by the river in gratitude for the power of knowledge you share. In your constant steadiness there are many lessons to learn. Oh river today I sing to thee in humbled gratitude to allow me this brief glimpse of your beauty. Of your wisdom. Of your might. Oh river.

September 7:

Yesterday was for the dreams. Sun warmed sage scented the air as we broke camp awaiting another day on the river. It was another day of my body being more capable than I believed. Another day facing my fears of rushing waters. Oh, how facing my doubts, conquering my fears has rewarded me. As we flowed with the current the moon followed like a close guardian, a companion. Stimulated by conversation and satiated in silence. As we flowed down river we spoke of great floods, of the magnitude of force that has created the wonders of landscape that surrounded us. How magical this realm of water and rock is. How mythical and now I am captured by its presence. Its presence encircles me, has allowed me into its embrace. High on the ridge tops are places often visited yet from the river perspective completely foreign. Anew do they gain my love. From the river I gain a peace I have not known. For the water sings its song of lapping gently against the shore. The peace of great power in steadiness. The calmness of consistency. As we floated along its surface we pass the places of my mother's past, the places so often relayed in stories. As we floated along its surface, we pass the trails my father built. I wonder where it is along this river passage, along the rock walls that my parents' paths crossed. For in that crossing I was destined to be. And as such has this canyon not always been at the depths of my being? As we floated on the surface we watched as otters played. As a bald eagle preened. As big horn sheep basked in the sun. In wonderment I wondered if this place is not a bit of my home.

**RANDI MOVICH**

## Canyon Wren

I am a canyon wren calling from a hidden spot.

Collector of millennial memories. Stardust. Smashed jewels spattered on inky skies.

Greenstone crumbles from ancient island chains, atoms woven into spider's lace.

Remnants of magma chambers, metamorphic subduction, oceanic lithosphere, collision of mantle and crust.

I am a canyon wren calling from a hidden spot.

My tiny trill tumbles precisely through cataclysmic canyon, echoing off layers of columnar cooling and lava frosting, dissolving to soil in the clutch of lichen and rain.

Rocky towers piled, outlined in violet sky high above river torment. Deep hurt threatens a pitch towards boulder wreckage. Serous diamonds beckon, riches of endless flow. My refrain intrudes. A bargain struck, retrace.

I am a canyon wren calling from a hidden spot.

Hackberry, willow, bunchgrass, chokecherry, alder and yellow pine camouflage my plumed tail. Bear, cougar, elk, deer, goat, sheep, coyote and wolf weave through brambles on fragile trails.

My voice guides blindly, a sweet siren's call to a tightly fibered nest, gently grasping your tiny dream fragments.

## Makara Moment

Let us linger at river's edge. Sunbaked and salty. Half mermaid, half packrat. Sea creature Makara, transporter of Ganga river goddess and sea god Varuna. We gather, admire, and pile tiny earthen gifts of speckled greenstone, burnt sienna, gray granite, sparkly rose quartz. We create art and kinship. Half-submerged in the sacred waters, motherhood stories flow.

A creative child instructed to take only five treasures in her pocket from the forest camp, empties socks stuffed, innocently exclaiming she did not break any rules. As her mother, you admire her out of the box thinking, refrain a smile, but deep down admire her creativity.

Our underwater castle grows. The colorful palette expands beyond audacious expectations.

Recalling our children stringing words beyond infinity. We muse over escape plans in our own homes to the closest flowing water. A shower, flushing toilette, face splashed. A few moments behind a locked door restores tiny remnants of who we were before.

Memories of pulling, stroking, squeezing; extracting milk from kindly goats until the bucket is rudely kicked, and we do in fact cry over spilled milk. Sustenance and nourishment lost. We cry harder.

A moment shared, a loss of self, a blossoming of another. No tug at our shirtsleeves, no authority in our voices. No errands or pickups. We sit so long our backs burn, hair crisp with sand and wind. The wake of a jet boat threatens to dislodge our pebble art. Unfazed, we add more. We pile, arrange, create and wonder when we will share the story of this moment. The sun lowers and reluctantly we rise, leaving mermaid behind, emerging with pockets dripping of stories and stones.

**ANDERS PACE**

## Layover Day

Layover day, Yay!
Not moving camp is so nice
We should do it twice!

## Whitewater

Oars still, heart pounding
Now! It's time to make the move
All forward, T-up!

## Coffee With a View

Golden and green hills
Shimmering Snake flowing free
Camp begins to stir

## ROBIN PACE

### Treat Rafts Like Lovers

Pump them up
speak sweetly
love them
rock hard and
soggy soft

Unzip them thoughtfully
and back up tenderly
go
s l o w l y.
Use lube when things get stuck

Avoid sharp
comments, rocks, and hooks.
Rub them down
run water
over every crack, fold, and crevice

Listen when they vent
learn to recognize
the difference
between a lil pressure release and
a full on hole.
Help patch them up if it's the latter

Linger together when you can.
Ride them hard
when you can't.
Hold on and
feel it, that
unnameable feeling
as you fall with gravity together

Treat yer raft like a lover.

SARAH PETRILLO

## My First Religion

My mother always left a spot for me in her garden. Not to grow roses or sprout tomatoes, but to dig. She set aside a trowel and some gloves, but I liked my bare hands better. Under the heat of the summer sun, the earth felt warm, damp from the wash of the morning sprinklers, and soft from the chicken manure that she spread in the spring. I would sit there in the dirt and dig until the rich brown soil turned cold and mixed with clay. There, I found the gold.

Earthworms.
Sprouting of holes by the dozens, squirming and glistening in the light of the sun. I would scoop them up in handfuls, watch them wiggle and feel their cool, silky bodies as they slipped through my fingers back into the earth. I would visit them for hours, mesmerized by their translucent bodies, by how they moved earth and blood through them.

Oh I was so delighted!
The ground was alive! How many secrets did it keep? How many spirits did it hold? Kneeling there, the earth was my altar, those worms my religion.

**BETH PIATOTE**

## 15 Questions to Ask a River

What is the worst thing about speedboats?

What is your real
name? What are the names
of your children?

Do you get tired of running all of the time?

How do the dams
feel, pressing on you like that?

Do the sturgeon tickle you?

Do you
remember me?
Do you
remember
my grandfather?

Does your body
ache when it floods?     Or do you
enjoy a good flood—a chance to exceed yourself
without apology?

Is it getting too hot?
Do the algae choke you?
Are your worried about the salmon?

Were you once a stream?
Were you once free?

## When I saw the stars

When I saw the stars I felt close to them. Always in the mountains, camping, no other light, they are close and clear. I saw the dense brightness of c'ewc'ewnim 'iskit, the ghost trail, which means I saw my ancestors. They feel close when I am here. When I saw the stars I felt loved by them. They are titilu, the Big Ones, the Ones who Came Before. When I saw the stars I saw many clusters I usually cannot see. Stars were falling and I heard the others exclaim, *Oh, there one goes!* When I was a child we would sleep outside with our cousins on our farm and we would watch for falling stars and make wishes. I was always wishing for a horse. A falling star is a light coming toward you. That is a promise, an omen, a sign. But a star glittering and fixed is also a promise, a light coming toward you, a great relative beaming down at you with love, wishing.

**REBECCA ROBINSON**

**PROMPT: Write from the perspective of a plant.**

**Cocklebur**

Got you again.

Spiky and sticky, I prick your finger and don't let go. You curse, offended. But you're also impressed. I can see it in your eyes. *You're so small,* you seem to say. *How do you do it?*

It's true, I punch above my weight. I go where I please, hitch a ride on your shorts. You don't notice me 'til you're fixing to leave. You pull me off. That'll leave a mark.

You look triumphant. Not so fast. Check your shirt sleeve. There they are. Meet my family. They're as strong as I am, and just as stubborn. Good luck getting rid of them.

You and your kind call me "invasive." Excuse me, but where did *you* come from? You've some nerve, barging in here, ripping us out by the roots, stuffing us in trash bags, abducting us from our riverbank home.

Go ahead, try and stop us. Uproot us, displace us, do your worst. I've seen it all before. You win this time, or so you think. But guess what? You missed a spot.

Back on the beach, a few dozen cousins of mine are hiding, biding their time until they find some unsuspecting creature's fur or fabric. Digging in with their tiny hooks, they won't let go until they reach their new home, whose sandy soil they will conquer, as they always do.

As for me? I'm alive and kicking and sticking (it) to the man. After you ditched me – nice throw, by the way – I made a beeline for your buddy's backpack. I'm halfway to Houston. The last laugh is mine.

So long, sucker.

## CLARK SHIMEALL

### Five parts on the river:

In my dreams, I see many things. My life is full of half-spun dreams, fragile filaments blowing in the breeze like spider's threads that I rush to gather up and follow, then drop. A web emerges– I think– despite my lack of direction. Still I cannot tell.

I went to the river and asked the water: who am I to be? What am I to do? The river gives no answer the way I crave, concrete, clear, determined. Instead it whispers hints, subtle intimations. I am not sure the river is qualified to be my advisor in matters of destiny and purpose.

I will tell the children that this is what I learned from the river: shut the fuck up. Listen. Let ego float with the current. Surrender. Work with the flow, not against it. Past, present, future are like bands of current, bouncing off wall or riverbed or braiding through each other, intermingled. All flow downstream.

Today, this is what I say to the river, and in saying this, I also say to myself: Be patient. Accept my failures and flaws. Bear my frantic scrabbling for purchase with grace. Forgive my ignorance, my fear, my smallness, my thoughtlessness. Grant me space and grace; give me the benefit of the doubt. I am trying, in my way. I am trying to be better.

In the future, I will tell the river: I am letting go of fear. I accept my place in the current. I do not yet need to know, nor can I know. I cannot rush what is not ready. I will build my house when I need it.
I surrender.

## Stream of Consciousness

I remember water
shifting frothing foaming a huge
whirling gyre
rainy falls
rainbowed glints in the mist thrown up
by pounding percussive deep
pouring over of water
I jump as a beginner does
up
not out
and then down
into a seam that seemed to
hungrily greet me
opened before me
white then green then
dark
dark because I always close my eyes underwater
for as long as I can remember
wanting to be not here
wanting to see light only when
it is safe to breath
but meanwhile I tumble
powerless panicked
pushed pulled
as the surface – *where? how?*
remains out of reach.

now the equator
diving down
kicker rock
ancient lava core soldered to the bay
pushing against my terrestrial body
its stubbornly
non-negotiable
lack of gills
chasing sea turtles along the coral garden
of purple orange green
stretched out in a vast vertical plain

into the receding dark
descending pinching nose to relieve my ears
screaming their stubborn warnings
I don't listen

sudden shift by rolling wave far overhead
swelling against the basalt
sunk below the raw force of it I feel
its crushing weight
instantly
forty feet of water sits on top of me
I have lost my buoyancy
the deep closes
I feel its pull
down
dark
my composure spills out in bubbles of breath
I swim
hungrily
frantically
eyes open
upwards toward the light

as the nights get crisp and long again
the fat, green river slides lazily past,
and summer starts to fade.

**There was a Great Flood:**

Many great floods, in fact. So many that the stories blended together and the people could no longer remember one from the next. Every generation had its flood, some two, and for a time people grew used to the idea. The floods came, and took many things, and left, and those that remained would come down from the high places to pick through a world reborn. This new world was blanketed by a fine, rich soil, and every summer when the earth grew dry and the winds came screaming across the basin there were great clouds of suffocating fertility that choked the sky. All this the people accepted. As the dust settled they moved back through the low country, discovering the new growth beginning there.

**debrief with pikuunin**

gosh, it was a:
summer of storms, summer of sun, summer of broken things - paddles, pfds, gopros, lenses, motorcycles, ankle, heart. summer of stumbles, flight and failure, unplanned lessons and humbling, summer of stomach-clenching insecurity. summer of lake landings and lessons. summer of elders. summer of ecstatic belonging and being in body and unexpected opportunity. summer of sage and gifts given and taken. summer of vinyl and venison, chest freezers scraped of stickers and thawed salmon at potlucks. summer of beautiful friends old and new and young and old. summer of attachments, of suffering, of striving outside of self. summer of the snake river, slimy and sinuous. summer of sowing seeds, of supple bodies intertwined. summer spent picking burrs from fur. summer of song on river and in longhouse, qáaws, cemíitx. summer of nimíiputimpt and español, australian english. summer of strava, fascia and blood and bone, muscling up mountain peaks. summer of settling, of finding place in the world, of gathering potential like fat, cell by cell.

JANIE TIPPETT

**RIVER MUSINGS… 2023 Fishtrap Outpost, Snake River**

September 6, 2023

7:00 a.m. Bernard Creek, Snake River… Hells Canyon, Idaho side, across from Wallowa County, Oregon…

Here is me, on a rocky shoreline, next to the river. Seated in a camp chair, feet resting on a large boulder. Wearing sandals without socks, clad in worn blue jeans and frayed T-shirt… *Alder Slope Run/Walk, Enterprise Summerfest 1999* printed on the front.

Here, in this place, downriver from Hells Canyon Dam… I am alone, having wandered off to write down my thoughts… Notebook in hand, pen poised, I listen to the suck and slurp of the swirling waters of the Snake… the distant roar of the rapids we experienced yesterday… the faint tinkle of laughter, as our crew (Winding Waters River Expeditions) relaxes between making coffee and setting out platters of sliced cantaloupe and grapes. Most of our River Writers have departed on a nature walk, led by our naturalist, Jan Hohmann. Hiking up-river, they will follow a steep, rocky trail, which will lead them to a bridge, that spans Bernard Creek… thence to the historic McGaffee Cabin… Jan will answer questions about the local flora and fauna… Since our classroom was this same cabin two years ago… in this same country where the Nez Perce wintered their own herds of horses and cattle… Their ancestral homeland… I contemplate this, as the sun makes its slow way down the opposite canyon wall to the Oregon shoreline… I'm in the moment, as Hells Canyon wakes up on this September morning. Slowly, the breathing canyon brightens, as the sun, rising in the East… makes its way down the west-facing rims… to the river…

I woke at dawn, rising up on a cot in my cozy tent, which was pitched in a sandy alcove, a slight rise from the river. My first morning here… I peeked outside the tent flap to where I was walled in by large river rocks, which appeared to be polished to an ebony-like finish… I imagined these enormous boulders held warmth from yesterday's heat… all the warmth I needed. I felt at home… this canyon enfolded me.

Only four more days and I will turn 90. I try not to think about this as my pen scribbles words... like the river rapids, my thoughts are three sentences ahead of my flying fingers... the sun creeps lower... I'm distracted, in a good way... molten gold reflected by the rising sun at my back... igniting rocky crags... reflecting on ever moving waters. Whitewater riffles rise above... shot with golden light. I hear the distant chatter of our youthful crew as they cook breakfast beyond the hackberry thicket which is located a few feet away from where my tent is pitched...

Earlier, as I made my way over a scatter of river rocks to the Groover, ammunition box in hand, a murder of crows, flying in pairs and singly, streamed overhead... I watched, curiously, as they settled noisily for a morning conference... I wondered if they meet every dawn, to confer about which camp site offers the best breakfast leavings? Then suddenly... a lovely waterfall of song... the descending call of the canyon wren... singing the morning fully awake... notes full of sheer joy... spontaneous, like a child's laughter... at that moment in time... I'm that little girl.

Having raised several crows and one blue jay, I speak their language... and feel most at home in the natural world. Akin to the Bluebird, Crow, Hawk and even the large boulder I rest my feet upon... I am river water... the dawn breeze that wanders down the canyon, the air I breathe, the cricket's chorus. In my old age... the river is my mate, my LOVER. I need no other... its watery words touch my very soul... soothes my aging body...

I gaze upriver... the sun has kissed the shore on the Oregon side of the Snake... I have no sense of time... I can better understand the Nez Perce now... being here... what is time? Certainly not 7:30 or 8:00 o'clock... simply when the sun rises.... warms me... and the rocks.... Seasons are marked by when the nine bark begins to rust on the canyon sides, and the Cottonwoods and Aspen thickets tremble with the first hint of gold. "Tis September, beginning of Indian Summer... When time we call a year, rolls around with its seasonal changes and we... like the rocks, the very canyon itself... age. Being born again in death... never dying, just morphing into eternity... which, Thank God, has never been defined... nor ever will be. We need mysteries... No google earth can give us an answer... some things are spiritual. Like those gentle spirit winds you feel but can't see... spirits live in the wind.

No one need be alone... Here, in Hells Canyon, one can feel the kinship with Mother Earth....the river itself is living water... sustaining life itself... like the great blue heron, poised to catch a fish... winging its way to a high point to feast... the river gives... also I remembered the osprey... we watched from our rubber rafts yesterday... the wild laws playing out... fish for the Heron... water for the fish...

The salmon-colored clouds have fled... the Snake is full of frothy bubbles... swirling around in the eddy... Clark, handsome, young rower of my raft... is announcing breakfast by blowing into some sort of ram's horn... Suddenly I'm hungry...

My soul is fed... now 'tis time to feed my body.

Note: written here at my Big Sheep Creek cabin not far from where Big Sheep Creek flows into the Imnaha River... Just a river drainage away from The Snake... both rivers run North... this piece was edited very little from those notes I scribbled on the banks of the Snake River at Bernard Creek... the same melodious crickets are chirping, the creek sings its song, and this October day is closing down...'Tis a golden October...fall is falling in the form of cottonwood and aspen leaves... floating on the silky waters of Big Sheep Creek... all of these waters will empty into the Snake at Eureka Bar... the Imnaha will carry my words onward to the mighty Columbia, thence to the ocean... a river of words... to mingle, evaporate and water the stars... Venus is especially bright in my canyon dawns... A kingfisher just flew up the creek... hunting trout... all's well...

## THE SLEEPING WOMAN...*Golden October on Sheep Creek Cabin*

October 16, 2023

Golden leaves, floating free, in sunlit air... silence, sudden cool breeze wanders down Big Sheep Creek Canyon. The morning sun burns over Middlepoint... Its warm rays bring on a hatch of aphids... insects, with minute transparent wings... filling the air... the ash tree... smoky blue, dead and dying aphids encircle its trunk... cover its leaves and branches with dull blue bodies... buzzing... in her ear... her nose... her hair, swarms of them... what does this mean?... unseasonably hot... Under the grape arbor above her front deck... a canopy of yellowing leaves.  New, green growth of canyon grasses... under layers of sun burnt summer...red/orange rose hips and flaming sumac... quivering cottonwood leaves, aspen thickets... blue skies brushed with mare's tails... one long contrail, far off hum of jet... Inside her cabin, screens block clouds of aphids... She's sleepy... nap time ...

The sleeping woman awakens from her dream... remembers:
Last Friday afternoon... across the creek... She and her friend, traipsing through waist high teasel and blackberry bramble... long thorny tendrils... tripping them up... avoiding downed fence where elk broke through... their trail leading to the old apple orchard... ruby red wind falls hidden in grass... shaking loaded limbs... laughing, scooping armloads of apples... filling their buckets... like bears... teenage kids, chums... delighting in simple pleasure, midst golden afternoon canyon silence.  Just the two of them... Adam and Eve... sharing an apple... crisp, clean, sweet juice running down their chins...

They weren't alone:   blue jays... crows... creek murmurings... Under rim rocks full of ancient caves, winter home to "the people" Ollocot's tribe... their presence felt... their spirits' warm breeze breath... basalt rims scraping the sky... Narrow river of blue... above their heads... color of Heavenly Blue Morning Glories...

Shared delight written there on that warm afternoon... golden moments... between two unlikely souls... who can't seem to terminate their friendship. Although they've tried... it endures... held together by memories... this sacred string of beads they wear... each bead a story...

soaked by the time they returned to the cabin, fire in the wood cook stove... warmed up the soup....

Scrabble games... warm apple pie...

In the Spring... walking her fence line... up and down canyon sides... pausing to silently gaze at unpeopled wildness around them... where bear, bobcat, cougar, deer, elk, coon, skunk, pack rat... crows, kingfisher... merganser ducks... mountain sheep... coyote, wolf, cottontail rabbit...canyon wren, rattlesnake... butterflies, owls, mice, bats, trout, steelhead... sumac, hackberry, elderberry, syringa... apples, plums, walnuts... persimmon, sage, cactus, apricots. Peaches... pears... tomatoes... black eyed Susans... grapes... English elms... aphids and yellow jackets listened to their stories and silences... Angels all around...

From her rocky skyline bed the Sleeping Woman smiled... remembering her own golden moments... before turning to stone.

Note: Across from my cabin... the shape of a woman sleeping on her back... gazing at the sky... can be seen... She has long hair, and you can see her chin and forehead... and her body stretched out in repose. At her feet is a stone statue of a hawk or eagle... forever perched, as if guarding her... Every Spring, a pair of eagles nests beneath her... in the crags... and raise their young... it is a sacred place... my friend and neighbor named her the SLEEPING WOMAN... and gave her to me as a gift... thanks, Ken and Maggie... The stone sleeping woman forever sleeps on the skyline of a steep canyon... near the settlement of Imnaha... which was a great wintering place for the Nez Perce.

# ELLEN WATERSTON

## Suture Zone
*What I learned about the formation of Oregon*
*and Hells Canyon while floating the Snake River.*

One hundred million years ago—rifts, flames, fusions, an explosive
collision of a floating tropical island! After drifting across the ocean
of Panthalassa, the micro-continent rafts raucously ashore and in a fiery
display glues itself to what's called Idaho today. Who knew!

To blunt the impact of this forced union, the island bride dowers
her granitic groom with blazing seamounts, embroidered limestone,
terranes of shiny blue-green serpentine, and the promise of a mighty
river to flow along the uneven scar of the merger.

It's a vow kept more millions of years later when Lake Idaho's glacial
membrane ruptures. The rushing, roiling water stampedes the nascent
channel, tossing boulders, giant firs, anything near the suture as it gouges
the canyon from Hell deeper and deeper still.

It's a needed water route, if treacherous. The Indigenous are first to learn
the lyrics of the river's gyring songs, to dance their brave dugouts through
the drumming rapids—harvesting mollusk and fish, thanking Great
Spirit, the only one they believe can claim ownership of any of this…

until settlers, with oxen for legs, muskets for arms, prove them wrong,
force their will on the Native peoples, the wild water, the resistant land;
flog their mules to pull faster over hard times, their wives and children
to hurry rocks off the fields.

Now the river's free flowing songs are gone. Instead, laments: for what's
dead, for dry beds flooded only when love is artificially released, the torrent
of humans razing such places despite good intent—leaving no trace,
pulling weeds (one invasive pulling another).

The guide lifts her oars, lets the raft drift. "Notice," she whispers so not to
disturb anything, "along the canyon wall." She points to ragged stretch marks
in the water, whorls quarreling on the surface. "The suture's still active. See
how the river moves in strange ways here, like more is about to happen."

## Ode to Janet

There once was a botanist named Janet
who knew every plant on the planet
and when it came to river dress
she showed the glamping rest of us
that less is more, tents are a pest,
and staying close to the ground
in all things is best.


## Untitled

time of life
life in time
etched
on the basalt canyon face
and mine

# FURTHER READING

## Published Works by Writers from the 2023 Fishtrap Outpost on The Snake River in Hells Canyon

**Beth Ann Estock**
*Weird Church: Welcome to the 21st Century* by Beth Ann Estock and Paul Nixon
*Holy Living: Discernment: Spiritual Practices for Building a Life of Faith* by Beth Ann Estock

**Amelia Diaz Ettinger**
*Speaking at a Time,* Poetry book collection, Redbat Press, 2015
*Learning to Love a Western Sky,* Poetry Collection, Airlie Press, 2020
*Fossils on a Red Flag,* Chapbook, Finishing Line Press, 2021
*Self-Dissection,* Chapbook, The Poetry Box, October, 2023
*Between the Eye of the Lizard and the Moon*, Redbat Press pending publication, 2024
*These Hollowed Bones,* Sea Crow Press, April 2024

**Kelly Fine**
To read more of Kelly's writing, please email her at kellykinneyfine@gmail.com.

**Janet Hohmann**
*Wildflowers of Hells Canyon*, Lucky Marmot Press, 2022

**Beth Piatote**
*The Beadworkers Stories*, Counterpoint, 2019
Forthcoming books:
*Nez Perce Word for Shark*, Milkweed Editions (poems)
*Living with History: Notes on the Indigenous Everyday*, Norton (essays)

**Rebecca Robinson**
*Voices from Bears Ears: Seeking Common Ground on Sacred Land*,
University of Arizona Press, 2018
Selected articles:
For Terrain.org:
"Views from the Colorado Plateau: The Bears Ears in Two Histories,"
published August 4, 2016.
"Letter to America," published January 20, 2017.
For *Boom: A Journal of California* (published by the University of
California Press)
"Reading Kevin Starr: Can the California Dream be Redeemed?"
Published in the Winter 2013 print edition; published online February
9, 2014.


**Janie Tippett**
FOUR LINES A DAY  (the life and times of an Imnaha Ranch Woman)
originally published by Pika Press in 2005, now in its third printing
under Lucky Marmot Press;  Six volumes of JANIE'S JOURNAL (thirty-
one years of ranching life in Wallowa County Oregon, published by
Lucky Marmot Press,  came out in 2021 I think...not sure...also
TALKING ON PAPER, an anthology of Oregon letters and papers...plus
CRAZY WOMAN CREEK...women re-write the American West...Mariner
Books  Houghton Mifflin Company, Boston, New York, 2004.
The Six volumes of JANIE'S JOURNAL consisted of my 31 years of
being a columnist for Agri-Times N.W.  a newspaper that had a five-
state audience. I began writing the column in 1984.


**Ellen Waterston**
*Walking the High Desert, Encounters with Rural America along the
Oregon Desert Trail,* University of Washington Press, 2020
*Hotel Domilocos,* Moonglade Press, 2017
*Via Lactea, a Woman of a Certain Age Walks the Camino*, Atelier 6000,
2013
*Where the Crooked River Rises, A High Desert Home*, Oregon State
University, 2010
*Between Desert Seasons*, Wordcraft of Oregon, 2008
*Then There Was No Mountain*, The Rowman and Littlefield Publishing
Group, 2003

Recommended by Beth Piatote

"How to Not Write a Sonnet," (essay) in *The Art of Revising Poetry*, ed. Kim Stafford and Charles Finn, 2023

"Secondary Infection," (story) in *Evergreen: Grim Tales and Verses from the Pacific Northwest*, ed. Sharma Shields and Maya Jewell Zeller, 2021

"The Night Walk," in *Spark: The Magazine of Humanities Washington*, 2021 Issue 1

"Level 8 Risk," *San Francisco Chronicle*, 16Aug2020

No grid.  Eighteen people.  Four rafts.  Snake River.  Hells
Canyon.  Wallowa County.  Oregon.  Idaho.  USA.
North America.  Earth.  Universe.